Restoring Rest to Sleepless Nights

SCRIPTURES AND DEVOTIONS TO HELP WITH SLEEPLESS NIGHTS

Doreen and Bradley,
May the verses in this book be an
encouragement to each of your hearts.
I pray they will bring the reassurance
needed during challenging times.
In His Love,
Pam Koerner

PAM KOERNER

ISBN 978-1-0980-3167-1 (paperback)
ISBN 978-1-0980-3168-8 (digital)

Christian Faith Publishing, Inc.
832 Park Avenue
Meadville, PA 16335
www.christianfaithpublishing.com

Printed in the United States of America

Acknowledgments

To God Himself for the encouragement and peace He consistently provides from His Word during sleepless nights.

To Gary, my husband, for his patience with my many hours of writing and for his encouraging comments as he read the things God was teaching me.

To my parents, Jack and Aurelia Hall, who maintained faithful commitment to their Lord while they were still on earth. I especially appreciate the faith they evidenced during tough times that showed each of us girls how to trust God regardless of the circumstances.

To each of my children, Sherrie, Annette, Jeff, Tim, Kayla, and their spouses (Joseph and Kimberly) for their support and input. I especially appreciate Joseph and Tim's help with IT issues when my computer "had a mind of its own."

To my friends who read the devotionals and encouraged me to put them in print.

To my aunts, Janice Mumford and Nea Young, who read the devotionals and encouraged me to publish them. I especially appreciate their wisdom and practical suggestions.

Introduction

Restoring Rest to Sleepless Nights is the product of months of sleepless nights due to typical life issues coupled with the side effects of a new medication that caused literal twenty-four-hour-a day insomnia for six months. A change in doctors and medication finally brought relief for medicine-related insomnia. However, months of no rest magnified nighttime anxieties, casting feelings of despair over day-to-day difficulties that seemed to have no end.

The result was a chance to discover God's answers to the problems. When I finally took my hands off matters and decided to *really* trust God for the much-needed solutions, He faithfully gave reassurance and guidance from scripture. He frequently used others to reaffirm the very truths He had just revealed. Sometimes He gently reminded me of things I had known for years. Other times, He gave reassurance from scriptures I had never noticed. Often, He showed me things others had grasped but I had neglected.

My prayer is that you will

- be greatly encouraged by the scriptures themselves,
- be refreshingly reminded of things you've known for years but possibly forgot,
- discover new truths from scripture to address your deepest concerns, and
- grow in your own spiritual life at the pace God intended specifically for you.

May you truly discover the power God has to restore rest to every sleepless night, regardless of the cause(s). To God be the glory for what He has done and will do in your life!

Don't be afraid of sudden fear,
nor of the onslaught of the wicked when it comes;
for the Lord will be your confidence
and will keep your foot from being caught.
—Proverbs 3:25–26 (NASB)

It has been said that Jewish scholars believe "every word of sacred Scripture has 70 faces and 600,000 meanings" (Batterson 2010). While it should never be lifted from its context, the many "sides" of each word could explain why God's Spirit can use a verse to address a variety of issues and to calm the distresses of one's soul.

When I was one, I had an illness that left me unconscious with a 106-degree fever for three days. Doctors at Baylor in Dallas gave my parents little hope I would survive. God was merciful and spared my life, but as a result, I have a daily battle with hypoglycemia, which can cause blood sugar to drop too low. Although medication and strict diet control the problem, complications occur from time to time. There have been frightening nights during which I could scarcely wait to see daylight. Sometimes daylight brought no relief.

In the middle of one terrifying night, God showed me Proverbs 3:25: "Don't be afraid of sudden *fear*" (NASB) or "danger" (HCSB). You see, Satan delights in instilling sudden terror in our minds and spirits, hoping to take our focus off our loving Father, who is constantly available to help. Sometimes Satan uses the "onslaught of the wicked" to bear down on us, making us feel the weight of apparent defeat. However, note what God says: "The Lord will be your confidence and will keep your foot from being caught." Regardless of the intensity of what we are experiencing, God Himself promises to be our confidence and promises to prevent even a single foot from being caught.

It is essential to remember that despite the nature of our struggles, God is not the one trying to frighten us. That tactic strictly belongs to Satan. Consequently, we must choose ahead of time whom we are going to believe when times are tough and fear is overwhelming. That choice will determine who wins the battles of our mind and spirit when we are under attack.

When fear invades the darkest hours of night, remind yourself of our Father's loving command: *Don't be afraid of sudden fear/danger.* Regardless of what the circumstances "shout," God still has you in the palm of His hand, and He will never let go. Intentionally take your fears to Him, leaving them to be saturated with His powerful solutions. Let Him be your confidence and bring the needed peace as He protects your precious life.

Behold, Thou dost desire truth
in the innermost being,
and in the hidden part Thou wilt
make me know wisdom.
Purify me with hyssop, and I shall be clean;
wash me, and I shall be whiter than snow.
　　　　　　　　　　　—Psalm 51:6–7 (NASB)

"I wish I had ——! How could I have been so stupid!" Wrong decisions often cause us to toss and turn at night, mentally and emotionally kicking ourselves over and over. We lose sight of the fact that true victory comes from pleasing God alone. Nevertheless, we find ourselves measuring success by whether we meet men's expectations and gain their approval. Sleepless nights result as we worry over our failure to please people.

Society demands we compromise and abandon our beliefs to gain its approval. God (in stark contrast) offers freedom of choice within safe guidelines. Those guidelines encourage development of true character that is not afraid of what others think.

Psalm 51:6–7 says we are to maintain integrity and truthfulness "in the innermost being." When one's heart and mind are honest with God, He causes the hidden inner parts of our soul to know His wisdom. He also gives the added benefit of experiencing His cleansing power after failure. He thoroughly washes away all that we did wrong, allowing us to seize the opportunity to try again, restoring hope for tomorrow.

Unfortunately, many never discover this hope because of misconceptions that God is uncaring and unforgiving. Such thoughts stand in opposition to reality. Note what God says:

- "I have loved you with an everlasting love; therefore, I have continued to extend faithful love to you" (Jeremiah 31:3, HCSB).
- "For I am the Lord your God, who upholds your right hand, who says to you, 'Do not fear, I will help you'" (Isaiah 41:13, NASB).
- "Come to Me, all of you who are weary and burdened, and I will give you rest" (Matthew 11:28, HCSB).

Consider the following promises:

- "If we confess our sins, He is faithful and righteous to forgive us our sins and to cleanse us from all unrighteousness" (1 John 1:9, HCSB).
- "As far as the east is from the west, so far has He removed our transgressions from us" (Psalm 103:12, HCSB).
- "The Lord is compassionate and gracious, slow to anger and abounding in lovingkindness" (Psalm 103:8, NASB).

God knows we will sometimes fail, but unlike people, He is always ready to give us another chance. He offers a new start every morning, viewing us with new loving-kindnesses and compassions (Lamentations 3:22–23). The new opportunities God sets before us allow us to focus on His promises, *not* our inadequacies. The inner wisdom we gain from being truthful with God not only equips us to handle the challenges of the day, but it also enables us to have the clear conscience needed to truly rest at the close of the day.

When failure seems to consume our thoughts and emotions, we must remember that we have a loving God who is always ready to let us try again. Not only does He give us another chance, but He also stays with us to keep us safe and give us rest.

For I am the Lord your God, who
upholds your right hand,
Who says to you, "Do not fear, I will help you."
—Isaiah 41:13 (NASB)

Natural disasters, embarrassing failure, terminal illness, harsh ridicule, terrorist attacks, unexpected unemployment—the list of things we fear is endless. One's personal experiences result in a different set of "fears" for each person. Whether real or imagined, one must deal with those fears to have peace of heart and mind.

Overcoming fear necessitates clearly identifying and confronting each fear. Sometimes there is an actual physical threat while other times we anxiously anticipate perceived danger. Occasionally, fear of the unknown or fear of failure replaces more tangible fears. Often they cause us to lose precious hours of sleep as we struggle with what *might* happen.

Consider the story in Matthew 25, which tells of a man going on a long journey who trusted his possessions to his slaves. He gave each slave a different amount according to his abilities. Two of them doubled that with which they were entrusted. The other slave hid his, claiming he was afraid of what his master might do. He allowed his imagination to overturn reality, choosing to magnify the hardness of his master instead of acknowledging the reality of his goodness.

How often do we do the same to God? We focus on God's intolerance of sin, neglecting to give Him credit for His unconditional love, mercy and generosity. Although scripture tells us no less than 365 times to not be afraid (Gaultiere 2019), we ignore God's commands and His promises to help. Instead, we allow fear to hinder our productivity and limit our rest.

How do we move past fear and stubborn resistance to God? It begins with the choice to let God search our heart (Psalm 139:23–24) and cleanse us of all that is wrong (Psalm 51:10). Nothing is ever resolved apart from these two starting points. That includes overcoming fear. Note the result of God's cleansing: it results in a renewed "steadfast spirit." When we allow God's scrutiny and cleansing of our ways, He replaces fear with confidence that cannot be shaken. The result is renewed courage and strength for handling the persistent challenges of the day.

Take hold of God's Word and claim it as something He wrote specifically to you: "Do not fear, for I am with you; do not anxiously look about you, for I am your God. I will strengthen you, surely I will help you, surely I will uphold you with My righteous right hand" (Isaiah 41:10, NASB).

Reflect on His Word throughout the day and confidently trust what He says. He promises He will keep in "perfect peace" those whose mind depends on and trusts in Him (Isaiah 26:3). That "perfect peace" will allow you to relax, experiencing the sleep needed to face a new day.

The fear of the Lord leads to life;
so that one may sleep satisfied,
untouched by evil.
　　　　　　　—Proverbs 19:23 (NASB)

Have you noticed the direct correlation between our relationship with God and our ability to sleep? Legitimate health issues or life stresses often lie behind one's lack of sleep, but sometimes the lack of sleep is God's gentle way of telling us, "There is something we need to talk about."

When our relationship with Him is lacking, it can be a fearful matter as God rightfully addresses the situation. However, it can also be reassuring, comforting, and healing as God takes the initiative to lovingly draw us back to Himself. Such action on God's part merits a healthy, respectful fear of Him on our part. When we have a reverent fear of Him, He promises we will "sleep at night without danger" (Proverbs 19:23, HCSB) or "untouched by evil" (NASB).

When we fear God alone, we will not only have a secure earthly life and peaceful nights of rest, but we will also have life with Him throughout eternity (John 3:16). That is something no one else can offer, yet we waste emotional energy and hours of sleep worrying over things having no eternal value.

This *does not* mean fear of and obedience to God will make our lives problem-free; neither does it mean we can abandon a common-sense fear of certain things. Peter writes of the reality that the genuineness of our faith *will* be tested by various trials (1 Peter 1:6–7)—trials that often stir up worry and fear. Even Jesus Himself was tested and tempted in every way we are—including being afraid—yet He chose not to give in to any form of sin (Hebrews 4:15).

When we fear and respect God only, we *will* encounter trouble, but we will be able to face it with courage and hope because God promises *He* will trample and tread down our enemies (Psalm 60:12; 108:13). Regardless of the dangers that threaten us, we can lie down and sleep at night as we allow our all-powerful God to accomplish *all* things for us (Psalm 57:20).

"For the mountains may be removed and the hills may shake, but My loving kindness will not be removed from you, and My covenant of peace will not be shaken," says the Lord who has compassion on you" (Isaiah 54:10, NASB). When peace of mind and heart are elusive, trust God to give you *His* unshakable peace that will let you "sleep at night without danger," "untouched by evil."

And you will seek Me and find
Me when you search for Me
with all your heart.
　　　　　—Jeremiah 29:13 (NASB)

Behold, Thou dost desire truth
in the innermost being.
　　　　　—Psalm 51:6 (NASB)

Has anyone ever approached you, asking about your well-being only to let his/her mind promptly wonder elsewhere? The person's body language, eye contact, and verbal response tell you attention is anywhere but on your answer. You experience a social formality performed with gestures that seem to show no real interest in you.

Human nature finds it easy to judge such people. However, one cannot help but wonder how often we do the same to God. We ask Him something, but as soon as He begins to answer, our focus is anywhere but on His response. We say we want God's answer when we are not sincerely interested—at least not right now *or* not on *His* timetable.

Adequately and thoroughly dealing with things that trouble us and keep us awake involves purposing to be honest with ourselves and honest with God. Good intentions accomplish nothing, and insincerity undermines any relationship. If *we* do not appreciate people who show half-hearted interest, why should we expect God to put up with ours? Yes, He loves us unconditionally, but it takes commitment on both sides for a relationship to exist. We cannot wait till the hour of need and expect God to answer when we are not sincerely truthful with or interested in Him.

A medication I take requires a couple of months to reach a stable level. Once in its therapeutic range, the medication still must be taken day after day. I cannot wait till problems occur, take the medicine, and expect it to help. It only works when I constantly keep it in my system at the right level. As a result, whether I am asleep or awake, the medicine does its job.

The same principle applies to our relationship with God. We must maintain daily two-way communication with Him for things to be in balance day and night. As a result, we instantly have the help we need to handle life's challenges.

When spiritual attacks and sleepless nights come, assess the truthfulness of your innermost being. Ask, "Am I truly searching for God with my whole heart, obeying Him without question? *Or* do I acknowledge Him one minute and ignore Him the next, still expecting Him to do what I want?"

When we willingly invest in a relationship with our Lord, He will be available day and night to help with our battles. Scripture assures us He "is able to do exceeding abundantly beyond all that we ask or think" (Ephesians 3:20, NASB). Nurture your relationship with God and discover true rest as He blesses you "exceedingly and abundantly" beyond anything you could imagine.

Ask, and it shall be given to you;
seek and you will find;
knock, and it will be opened to you.
For everyone who asks receives,
and he who seeks finds,
and to him who knocks it shall be opened.
—Matthew 7:7 (NASB)

Do you lie awake revisiting and worrying over what to do to be successful? No doubt everyone would like to succeed, but what really makes a successful person? Success has many sides and angles. Society includes education, talent, intelligence, performance, productivity, and wealth as a few indicators of success. A mind-set of confidence and perseverance also plays a significant role in one's success. However, they are not among God's criteria. Consider what 1 Corinthians 13:1–3 (HCSB) says about one of God's "measures" for success:

> If I speak the languages of men and of angels, but do not have love, I am a sounding gong or a clanging cymbal.
> If I have the gift of prophecy, and understand all mysteries and all knowledge and if I have all faith, so that I can move mountains, but do not have love, I am nothing.
> And if I donate all my goods to feed the poor, and if I give my body to be burned, but do not have love, I gain nothing.

Obviously, one can be very capable and prosperous in his/her respective fields. However, the child of God must also sincerely demonstrate unconditional love. It does not matter what kind of success the world attributes to a person if he/she falls short of God's expectation to love one's neighbor (Leviticus 19:18). This leads one to ask, "How can I love those whose behavior and attitudes constantly undermine trust and nurture resentment? How can I love that mean-spirited boss, coworker, or family member?"

Matthew 7:7 holds the key: keep knocking and asking. In other words, keep praying and asking God to make the needed changes. That includes allowing Him to deal with any personal hardness of heart, replacing it with His kind of love. Unfortunately, this is more easily said than done, so how can it be accomplished?

- The starting point is always with *God* and *oneself*: "Search *me*, O God, and know *my* heart; try *me* and know *my* anxious thoughts; and *see if there be any hurtful way in me*" (Psalm 139: 23–24, NASB).
- Next, ask for His help: "Create in *me* a clean heart, O God, and renew a steadfast spirit within *me*" (Psalm 51:10, NASB). By faith (Hebrews 11:6), trust Him to not only forgive and cleanse you (1 John 1:9) but to also replace your lack of love with His love (1 Corinthians 13).
- Again, keep "knocking"—persevere as you pray (Matthew 7:7).
- When unloving thoughts and emotions return, immediately take them back to Christ, leaving them with Him (2 Corinthians 10:5).

Take comfort in the fact that God will answer when you ask. Furthermore, Jesus has been exactly where you are. He knows how to help you love unlovable people. When it is difficult to sleep, search your heart, allowing your Lord to replace your lack of love with His concern and compassion. Then you can rest, confident you are headed toward God's kind of success.

I rise before dawn and cry for
help; I wait for Your words.
My eyes anticipate the night watches,
that I many meditate on Your word.
—Psalm 119:147–148 (NASB)

I rise before dawn and cry for help; I
have put my hope in Your word.
My eyes stay open through the watches
of the night that I may meditate
on Your promises.
—Psalm 119:147–148 (NIV)

*P*erspective has the power to change negative situations to positive. One can fix his/her gaze on a problem, focusing on all its negative aspects, *or* he/she can acknowledge the situation and look for an opportunity.

No doubt the eagerness of David's enemies to attack caused him to lie awake from time to time, facing the reality of all the negative things taking place around him. However, Psalm 119:147–148 indicates David assigned purpose to his nighttime hours. It notes that before dawn, he cried to God for help. He did not allow dawn to arrive without first spending the darkest hours of night crying out to his Father.

David was not content just spending time with God early in the morning. Verse 148 (NASB) says he "anticipated" the night watches. In other words, he looked forward to those sleepless nights, viewing them as an opportunity instead of an inconvenience. He seized them as a chance to meditate on God's word and his Father's promises.

Although he experienced discouragement, depression, distress, and despair, David openly acknowledged his feelings throughout the book of Psalms. While he was honest in expressing them, he also noted how he was going to handle them. Without fail, he stated time after time that he was going to take refuge in his God, who could take care of any enemy and any situation. David knew this was essential to controlling his emotions and crucial to securing a proper perspective on life.

What can we learn from David's example?

- When problems come, focus on the opportunities, not the problem.
- Be honest about how it makes you feel; document it if needed.
- Purpose ahead of time to always trust your God. Document how you will show your trust in Him.
- Assign purpose to your sleepless nights. Pray or meditate on scripture. Memorize scripture relevant to your problem(s).
- Take hold of the new day by baring your heart to the Father before dawn arrives.
- Above all, be still and listen to your Heavenly Father. He has your best interests at heart and wants to give you His kind of victory over your problems.

When sleepless nights come, take control of the situation. Be aggressive and intentional about spending every waking hour in the presence of your Lord. He will reward your determination with new depths of freedom that will bring the rest you need.

In peace I will both lie down and sleep,
for Thou alone, O Lord,
dost make me to dwell in safety.
—Psalm 4:8 (NIV)

Day after day, anxiety and fear tend to be the primary "fuels" that ignite insomnia. When coupled with being alone, they can intensify a stifling sense of hopelessness. Uncertainties about the future add to one's increasing inability to relax and sleep. Life's circumstances or physical issues compound matters, bringing additional reminders that things are not "okay." Helplessness and despair increase. Things snowball, and everything that could go wrong does, leaving feelings of worthlessness and insecurity.

We know with our minds that God can help; nevertheless, we become weary and vulnerable when problems escalate, and we do not clearly see an answer. We feel bombarded and wonder how God can possibly resolve the overwhelming chaos. Our physical and emotional energies become depleted, leaving us in a state of desperation. What can we do?

Over and over, we find our greatest battle is with the thoughts of our mind. We attempt to weigh facts to figure out a course of action. We forget that human effort and reasoning can sometimes stand in the way of discovering *God's* answers. In our haste to find answers, we overlook the fact that simply trusting God is all that is necessary (Hebrews 11:6).

David's faith gives a perfect example of what to do when life is out of control, moving rest beyond our grasp. First, he chose his course of action. Next, he affirmed his trust in God, alone.

Finally, David put his plan in writing: "I will lie down in peace and sleep, for Thou alone, O Lord, dost make me to dwell in safety."

David told his mind and spirit, "I will lie down in peace and sleep," no questions asked. That was going to be his course of action. Why? He had full confidence in his loving God.

Our loving Lord has not changed (Hebrews 13:8), and He knows our needs. He watches over the tiny sparrow, *and* He watches over us (Matthew 10:29–31)! He owns the cattle on a thousand hills (Psalm 50:10) and has unlimited resources to "supply *all* our needs according to His riches in glory in Christ Jesus" (Philippians 4:19).

God knows our need for physical, spiritual and emotional rest, *and* He knows what "things," situations or relationships need to be fixed. That is why He tells us to be anxious for *nothing*, making our requests known to Him with a spirit of thanksgiving for what He is going to do (Philippians 4:6).

One evening in the middle of some very trying circumstances, my husband and I called my dad to ask his counsel. As our conversation ended, Dad said, "God has never failed anyone and He's certainly not going to start with you!" The same is true for you. God has never failed anyone, and He is not going to start with you. Regardless of what is going on, lie down in peace and sleep as God protects every aspect of your precious life.

Cast your burden on the Lord,
and He will sustain you;
He will never allow the righteous to be shaken.
                         —Psalm 55:22 (NASB)

One of the people whom I most loved and admired was Pap, my grandpa. Before I was scarcely old enough, he began teaching this city girl how to fish. I was not particularly crazy about fishing because I did not like the "fishy" smell. Nevertheless, if Pap thought it was something I needed to learn, I was most eager to try.

Pap would break off a cane pole, cut the end with his knife, attach a fishing line, secure a hook and off we would go. He had the perfect place to dig worms or catch grasshoppers. This was quite a feat for a youngster who preferred reading to catching "critters!" He would often laugh at my hesitant and sometimes futile attempts to retrieve the bait, encouraging me to keep trying till I succeeded.

When we settled on the bank of his fishing pond, he helped me load my hook with those gross worms and grasshoppers. He showed me by example how to cast my fishing line and bait onto the water. Once I had a "feel" for what I was supposed to do, he left me to do my own casting. Next came his most important lesson—be still and wait.

Psalm 55:22 reminds me of the lessons learned from Pap. First, I had to practice casting my own fishing line if I was to learn how to do it. The same is true of our spiritual lives. We must cast our own burdens upon the Lord; others cannot do it for us.

Just as patience is necessary to catch fish, patience is vital to receiving God's answers. When we have cast our burdens upon the Lord, we must not be hasty in wanting to "reel in" the answer. While we wait, He will sustain us, not allowing us to be shaken.

Although his physical life was in danger, Jesus lay asleep in the middle of a storm (Mark 4:35–41), casting the burden of His safety on His Father. Jesus knew in the depths of His spirit that His Father would sustain Him and not allow Him to be shaken. We, too, can sleep during the storms of life, knowing God is in full control as He looks out for our well-being.

When we cast the burdens of our heart on the Lord, He will calm our storms. Furthermore, He will provide solutions when we wait on the perfect timing of His answers.

Never be afraid to sleep in the middle of life's storms. Regardless of the turbulence and chaos around us, God Himself will never allow His children to be shaken.

"For I know the plans I have for you,"
declares the Lord, "plans for welfare
and not for calamity,
to give you a future and a hope."
—Jeremiah 29:11 (NASB)

Two months had passed since beginning a new medicine that was working beautifully. I had never felt better. For once, I felt I might be able to experience "normal" life like other people. However, I awakened one morning to find a small rash I had not previously seen. Thinking it was due to the extreme heat, I dressed in lightweight clothing, going about the business of the day.

That night, I noticed the rash was more intense and rapidly spreading. It was Friday night, and I was several hours from my doctor in Dallas. The doctor on call advised dropping the new medication and returning to the previous prescription which I had tolerated. He said if the rash didn't improve, see our family doctor as soon as possible.

When I saw our family doctor, his years of experience immediately recognized a fixed allergic reaction to the new medication. It had the potential of being fatal if they could not get the reaction to reverse. He promptly began shots and prescribed four different antihistamines to take simultaneously every four hours, hoping to break up the reaction.

Two weeks later, the massive rash began to go away. Meanwhile, the discomfort coupled with the reality that the reaction could be fatal brought sleepless nights. Whether I lived or died, I needed reassurance from God Himself. During one of the many sleepless nights, I discovered Jeremiah 29:11 for the first time. Although it was initially given to the children of Israel to give them hope, God's timeless principles hold true for all His children. It says God knows the plans He has for us—they are plans for our welfare, not calamity, so He can give us a future and give us hope.

Despite seeing no progress up to this point, I had to choose to believe or not believe God's promise. Although the immediate physical "disaster" seemed irreversible, the verse reassured me God had my well-being in mind, offering words of hope that there *would* be a future for my life. With this reassurance, I was finally able to lie down and sleep despite the discomfort and despite seeing no improvement.

God is not a mean ogre looking for ways to make us miserable. He sincerely loves and cares about us. He *wants* to give us peace of mind so we can truly rest and *know* in the depths of our being there *is* a future and there *is* hope.

Regardless of how things appear, choose to believe God, resting in the fact that you *do* have a future and you *do* have hope for the days ahead. It might not happen the way we expect; nevertheless, we can count on God to help us through whatever lies ahead on earth and in eternity.

The Lord will sustain him upon his sickbed;
In his illness, Thou dost restore him to health.
                                        —Psalm 41:3 (NIV)

When I was quite young, my grandmother often sat me on the piano bench near her rocker as she crocheted. She encouraged me as I learned to play the piano, patiently letting me experiment while she taught me how to listen for mistakes. She lay the foundation for later teachers who taught me what it meant to sustain a note.

The above verse reminds me of what they said: if you are holding the note down, even when the sound fades, you are technically still sustaining the note. The same concept can be applied to our relationship with God. When it appears God is no longer holding or sustaining us during difficult situations or illnesses, we must remind ourselves of His promise in Hebrews 13:5: "I will *never* desert you, nor will I *ever* forsake you." Although we might not have tangible or audible signs that God is still working, He *is* still supporting, sustaining and holding us—even when it seems He is not there.

One summer, some friends and I decided to learn to swim for the sakes of our young children. Several of us were a "substantial size" and were afraid the water would not hold us. Consequently, when our first lesson was to learn to float, we were convinced we were doomed to drown. Our teacher was a good friend. She laughed and told us, "There is a principle of physics that says [in layman's terms]: 'The bigger you are, the better you float.' That is why huge ships can easily float on the water—even in the middle of a storm."

In a sense, the same is true of our spiritual lives: the greater our trust in God, the better we will "float" when we encounter the storms of life. The bigger the problem, the better it can be handled. The key is allowing it to rest in God's hands, not ours.

God is always available to sustain us in times of illness and in times of trouble, but we must relax and let Him hold the massive weight of all that is happening. Sometimes we will see Him restore our physical health on earth. Other times we will be blessed with eternally perfect health by getting to go home to heaven. Either way, we can have every confidence that our Father is holding us safely and securely as He restores our health. When the "music" in life fades and can no longer be heard, remember that we have a faithful and loving God who is sustaining us even when it seems no one is there.

For thus the Lord God, the Holy
One of Israel, has said,
"In repentance and rest you shall be saved,
In quietness and trust is your strength."
—Isaiah 30:15 (NASB)

Jonathan Cahn's book *The Harbinger* skillfully compares Israel's defiance of God with America's. It prompts one to wonder if current events evidence the inevitable—that God has finally had enough of America's indifference to Him. The week I finished the book, five million people along the East Coast lost power, homes, transportation, food, etc. due to unexpected storms. That was more than the three million affected by the devastation of Hurricane Katrina.

Today storms are pounding the East Coast, causing massive mudslides. Once again, fires rage out of control in the Midwestern and Western states, destroying entire communities and thousands of acres of land. Severe drought plagues crucial farmland in the Central United States. Gulf Coast states are flooded due to torrential rains that destroyed entire neighborhoods and towns. Tornadoes have destroyed homes and businesses throughout the land. Many maintain they will "pull themselves up by their bootstraps" and try again. Seldom does one see evidence of people realizing the need to seek God and His help rebuilding their lives.

One should not automatically attribute the catastrophes to man's sin, but neither can the connection between the two be ignored. The severity, consistency and magnitude of our national disasters prompt me to realize the need to personally examine my own heart and repent of sin. Second Chronicles 7:14 (NASB) says, "If… My people who are called by My name humble themselves and pray, and seek My face and turn from their wicked ways, then I will hear from heaven, will forgive their sin and will heal their land." Refusal to do so has devastating consequences for individuals and nations. How does this affect one's ability to rest?

When one wrestles night after night with catastrophes and losses while holding tightly to indifference toward and independence from God, no lasting solutions can be found. Immorality and callousness grow, increasing the spiritual battles that contribute to lack of rest. Couple this with dependence on oneself to fix life's problems and one cannot help but be overwhelmed.

According to a CBS news report on August 29, 2013, nearly nine million Americans use sleep aids. An estimated fifty to seventy million suffer from sleep disorders or sleep deprivation. An estimated $41 billion was spent on sleeping aids and remedies in 2015. A 2016 study estimates 164 million Americans struggle at least once a week to get the recommended seven hours of sleep while another study shows less than one-third get the recommended seven to nine hours of sleep per night ("Consumer Reports," *Why Americans Can't Sleep,* January 14, 2016).

Such statistics clearly evidence a growing problem. While a multitude of things are legitimate contributing factors, spiritual matters are seriously disregarded. God says, "In *repentance* and rest you shall be saved, in quietness and trust is your strength" (Isaiah 30:15, NASB). When we take ownership of what we have done wrong and choose to do things God's way, rest will no longer be elusive. God's kind of quietness and peace will make sleepless nights a thing of the past as He works to restore order to our lives.

Blessed be the Lord who daily bears our burden,
the God who is our salvation.
God is to us a God of deliverances,
and to God the Lord belong escapes from death.
—Psalm 68:19–20 (NASB)

Life changes can bring the joys of new beginnings and exciting opportunities. However, they can occasionally be unwanted changes that bring disheartening outcomes, many of which contribute to sleepless nights. Loss of independent living, significant relationships, financial security, social freedom, job satisfaction, and physical health are but a few of the factors that can bring unexpected, unwelcome changes. How can one realistically deal with such disruptions?

For myself, I must begin by being honest about what I am thinking and feeling. Next, I have to intentionally refocus my thoughts and emotions Godward. That includes *thoroughly* believing and having faith in what God says. Psalm 68:19 says He *daily* bears our burden. I must hold on to the fact that God already picked up the weight of my burden *before* I awakened to begin the day. That includes the weight of my anxieties over unexpected events.

Perhaps you are thinking, *But today's difficulties are different from what God is used to handling. We live in an entirely different day and age. He does not really understand.*

Such a view truly shows our ignorance about the only true and living God who not only made *all* things but by whom all things in the universe hold together (Colossians 1:16–17). *He* is the sole giver of all our intellect. He knows more about today's issues than all mankind combined. He no doubt chuckles at our modern-day advances because they are so inferior to what they could be.

Today's challenges are not new to God. Consider the following Bible characters who experienced some of our same frustrations:

- Loss of independence resulting in frustration over not being able to come and go as one pleases (Joseph, Daniel, Paul and Silas)
- Failed relationships due to lack of commitment to God's standards (Hosea and Gomer; David and Bathsheba)
- Business failures due to unfaithful colleagues (Jesus, as a spiritual entrepreneur, had disciples who ultimately denied Him despite all they witnessed.)
- Lifestyle change due to being a full-time caregiver (Ruth and Naomi; Christ Himself as He cared for the disciples and multitudes)
- Burnout or emotional breakdown (Elijah)
- Extended illness (blind man by Pool of Siloam, woman with blood disease)

The same God who worked in miraculous ways in men and women's lives throughout history is the same God who wants to work in our lives today. He alone has the power to sustain us through or deliver us from any situation.

When God's answer is not what we expect, it never negates God's love for us and His ability to help. He is *not* powerless over and clueless about our circumstances and needs. Instead, He is at work to bring about the course of action that will best benefit us and those around us. Remember, He was fully aware of today's events before man even existed. Regardless of the nature of your troubles, resolve to let your loving Father carry *all* your burdens so you can find true rest.

The Lord is my light and my
salvation; whom shall I fear?
The Lord is the defense of my
life, whom shall I dread?
Though a host encamp against
me, my heart will not fear;
Though war arise against me, in spite
of this I shall be confident.
—Psalm 27:1, 3 (NASB)

Over and over we read about David consistently facing strong enemies who threatened his life. Some days, they were greater in number than others. However, David learned and lived the approach of turning to his Lord instead of focusing on his enemies. He chose to stand firm, resolving to be confident in God's ability to take care of him.

Today, many feel life's difficulties are insurmountable. About the time peace comes, another attack begins. Confusion and frustration set in over another war with life. An internal battle rages over whom to believe: God or the attacker.

When the children of Israel wandered in the wilderness for forty years, they were at war with life. They not only lacked direction and purpose, but they also needed food, shelter, clothing and protection. They ignored the fact that their circumstances were consequences they brought on themselves. Despite their rebellion, God caused their clothes and sandals to never wear out (Deuteronomy 29:5ff). When enemies rose against them, God gave His children victory. With every turn of events, He was right there to help.

Nevertheless, the children of Israel remained indifferent. They constantly grumbled, intentionally ignoring all God's provisions. What a mirror of America today! God has abundantly blessed our nation, yet we are ungrateful and defiant, desiring to remove God from our lives.

Like the Israelites, we have not been sorry for or repentant of the sins we have committed or the evil we have embraced. We scoff at things God says are nonnegotiable (e.g., placing our faith in Christ, obeying the Ten Commandments, being holy as He is holy, refusing to embrace immorality, etc.). Nevertheless, God still loves us, offering repeated chances to repent and return to Him (2 Chronicles 7:14, 1 John 1:9). Despite our indifference, He still desires to forgive us and give us new direction.

The healing process for today's wars with life begins with turning away from sin and intentionally turning back to God. This isn't a onetime event. It is a day-after-day discipline that enables us to maintain a right heart before God. When our hearts are right with God, we can be confident He will defend and protect us.

Like David, we need to focus *first* on our Lord, *not* our problem(s), praising God for who He is. Next, we must firmly acknowledge the fact that we have no need to fear. Even if we face outright war, we can remain confident in what God is going to do. Our loving Father is personally and powerfully standing guard to protect our lives. Therefore, we can rest at night, knowing we are surrounded with eternal protection that nothing can destroy.

How precious also are Thy thoughts to me, O God!
How vast is the sum of them!
If I should count them, they would
outnumber the sand.
When I awake, I am still with Thee.
—Psalm 139:17–18 (NASB)

Many of us are blessed with affirming people who see the best in us despite our flaws. Others of us have significant people who focus on our imperfections, reminding us of our inferiorities and/or inabilities. They make us feel as if we are a failure with no future. We "buy in" to their lies that we are of no value to anyone. We conclude that we deserve to be ostracized from and rejected by society. We spend day and night agonizing over our seemingly final defeat.

If there is no hope for the defeated, Jesus would not have taken the time to help the man living in the tombs in the region of the Gerasenes (Mark 5:1–20, HCSB). Society forced the man to live outside the town because of his behavior. "He often had been bound with shackles and chains but had snapped off the chains and smashed the shackles. No one was strong enough to subdue him. And always, night and day, he was crying out among the tombs and in the mountains and cutting himself with stones" (Mark 5:4–5, HSCB).

In spite of all that was wrong with the man, when he saw Jesus from a distance, he ran and knelt down before Him, crying out with a loud voice, "What do You have to do with me, Jesus, Son of the Most High God? I beg You before God, don't torment me!" (Mark 5:6–7, HCSB). One could argue the man's response showed the demon, not the man, recognized Jesus. The man had been demon-possessed so long that the unclean spirit controlled the man's behavior and his identity. However, in the presence of the Almighty Savior, the unclean spirit knew it was powerless because of the man's great value to God Himself.

When Jesus commanded the demon to come out (Mark 5:8), He asked his name. The unclean spirit said, "My name is Legion… because we are many" (Mark 5:9). Despite their number, Jesus had *total* power over *all* of them. The demons knew they had to leave the man, so they begged to enter a nearby herd of pigs. When the unclean spirits left, people found the man dressed and in his right mind.

Do others doubt the reality that *you* can change? Do *you* doubt Jesus can change a broken and shattered life? The same God who shows power over thousands of demons wants to show the same power in your life. His thoughts about you are precious and out-number the grains of sand.

When you awaken in the middle of the night, heartbroken and defeated, He is right there with you (Psalm 138:18). Give Him the chance to heal your hurts and help you reach your full potential. Never give in to society's rejection. Nothing is impossible for your loving Father who values your life and wants you to succeed. When sleeplessness invades the night, rest in the fact that you are surrounded by the love of God and the protection of His power. He will restore the soundness and peace of mind needed for full and complete rest.

Even before they call, I will answer;
while they are still speaking, I will hear.
                    —Isaiah 65:24 (HCSB)

They were nothing but plain ordinary women, but when they got together to pray, God listened. They did not put on airs; neither did they boast about their faithfulness to pray. When there was a need, they quietly and sincerely brought their heartfelt requests to their Heavenly Father, trusting Him to answer according to His will.

One day, I shared my concerns about our five-year-old son with the ladies. One of his eyes turned to the inside while the other deviated to the outside. The pediatrician recommended allowing time to see if the problem would correct itself. However, as time passed, it became obvious something would need to be done. The ladies began to pray God would provide the right doctor.

A few weeks later, we were able to get an appointment with a pediatric ophthalmologist in Dallas, Texas, known for successfully working with problems in young children's eyes. When the doctor checked our son, he said, "I have seen children born prematurely with one problem or the other, but never both problems in the same child. With your permission, there is someone whom I would like to consult. He flies to our state once a month from Washington, DC. He is literally the world's top specialist in dealing with muscle issues concerning the eye. I would like to see if he would check your son and see what can be done."

The world-renowned doctor not only saw our son to give advice, but he also flew halfway across the United States to supervise the needed surgery. God not only heard the ladies' prayers, but He set things into motion to literally bring the best man in the world to help.

We do not have to be someone special to receive God's help. He is eager to hear the prayers of plain, ordinary people when they take the time to pray. He is so interested in our requests that before we ask for help, He is already at work to answer. Furthermore, He has the resources to bring whomever He chooses into the picture to make the answer a reality.

When you have any concerns that bring sleepless nights, take them to your Heavenly Father who will answer when you take time to ask. Also share your concerns with godly friends who will pray with you because "the prayer of a righteous man is powerful and effective" (James 5:16, NIV).

Never doubt the power of prayer and God's willingness to answer. While we must take the initiative to take our requests to Him, we can be confident that He is already at work to provide the answer. He literally wants to give us His best, and He alone can make that happen.

Do not call to mind the former things,
or ponder things of the past.
Behold, I will do something new.
Now it will spring forth;
will you not be aware of it?
I will even make a roadway in the wilderness,
rivers in the desert.
                    —Isaiah 43:18–19 (NASB)

Each of us needs a fresh start from time to time simply due to being human. Nighttime reflections often affirm our daytime realizations that we simply need to start over and try again.

Other times, unwarranted and unjustified mistreatment by others forces us to make unplanned changes. Sometimes we must intentionally turn loose of the past, walk away and never look back. That does not mean we ignore what we have learned from our mistakes or mistreatment; but it *does* mean we can begin again when we have done everything possible to be reconciled with God and man. When those conditions are met, we have total freedom to move on, leaving the past behind.

Beginning again carries a realistic measure of fear, but we should never let it keep us from experiencing the new things God has planned. The starting point must be a decision to "not call to mind the former things." Next, we need to couple that with disciplining the mind to "not…ponder [or purposely reflect on] the things of the past" (v. 18). Then our new beginning will start to unfold. These steps are essential because embracing and reflecting on past defeats only breed fear over future failure. Looking at the past also turns the focus onto *our* inadequate human efforts, not God's limitless power.

It is important to note Who carries the weight in the process of beginning again. God says, "Behold, *I* will do something new. Now it will spring forth" (v. 19). When everything seems to fall apart around us, we are not "washed up" or "finished." Instead, God Himself stands ready to do something new in our lives.

The situation may seem unbearably bleak, but note what else God says: "I will even make a roadway in the wilderness, rivers in the desert" (v.19). We may feel as if we have been left to find our way in a barren wilderness, but God says He will make a roadway—not just a path, but a firmly established roadway to help us make it through our wilderness of defeat. Furthermore, He says He will give us *rivers* in the desert so that no matter how dry we are, an abundance of refreshment will be available to replenish our weariness.

Do not let past failures or overwhelming circumstances determine the outcome of your future or steal your rest at night. Remember that God Himself has something new in store not only for the days ahead, but also for the present moment. "*Now* it will spring forth; will you not be aware of it?" (v.19). Never hesitate to allow God to hand you His new beginning. It is ready for you right now.

A man's heart plans his way,
but the Lord determines his steps.
—Proverbs 16:9 (HCSB)

Do you ever plan your day around things that must be done or your finances around bills that must be paid only to have everything change? Does frustration set in when daily responsibilities are replaced with emergencies? Do unexpected changes or interruptions occasionally throw your day into disarray?

No doubt all of us have life "rearranged" from time to time, upsetting our attempts at responsible time management and job performance. We even wrestle at night, worrying over what we should or could have done. We lie awake perceiving ourselves as failures. What can be done to reject feelings of defeat and maintain calmness of spirit when things do not go the way we planned?

Proverbs 16:9 says, "A man's heart plans his way, but the Lord determines his steps." When a person sincerely wants God's will in his/her life, there will be a calm realization that "it is okay when things do *not* go my way because my Heavenly Father is guiding my steps with my best interests in mind."

God does not manipulate us, but He surrounds His children with protection because of the evil that *does* try to persuade our decisions. Psalm 91:11 (HCSB) says, "For He will give His angels orders concerning you, to protect you in all your ways." Psalm 34:7 also says, "The angel of the Lord encamps around those who fear Him and rescues them."

When things are chaotic and appear out of control, realize God has not abandoned you. In fact, He is very much at work to safely help you succeed at that to which He has called you. Note *who* He says will accomplish His purposes for your life: "Faithful is He who calls you, and *He* also will bring it to pass" (1 Thessalonians 5:24, NASB).

Choose to "tune out" Satan's nagging accusations and rest in the fact that your loving God is concerned about the smallest detail of your life. He is at work to give you success, and *He* will do what is needed to enable you to accomplish His plans.

Dr. Steve Maraboli has a quote that says, "Every time I thought I was being rejected from something good, I was actually being re-directed to something better" (Maraboli 2013). Give God the freedom to turn any rejection to redirection throughout the day so you will have the joy of experiencing His best for your life. This will allow you to rest at night, knowing the day ended as it should because you allowed God to direct your steps.

But He said to me, "My grace is sufficient
for you, for [My] power is perfected in [your]
weakness." Therefore, I will most gladly
boast all the more about my weaknesses, so
that Christ's power may reside in me.
                                    —2 Corinthians 12:9 (HCSB)

Has it happened again? Did you fail at something for the third, fourth or fifth time (maybe more) only to find yourself lying awake, chiding yourself once again over what you *should* have done? *Or* has that persistent health problem raised its wearisome head, again limiting your activity? Whatever the situation, we often let defeat loom heavily over our heads when our human weaknesses surface.

God in His infinite wisdom knows the flaws in our character and the physical battles we encounter. While He never interferes with our choices, He stands ready to help us pick up the pieces and move on with life.

The apostle Paul writes that God's grace is *sufficient*—it totally provides exactly what is needed. How can this happen? The perfectness of God's power readily matches our failures and weaknesses. He replaces them with His strength, allowing Christ's power to reside in and rest on us. Consequently, our greatest weakness becomes our strongest point as the weakness melts and dissolves in the presence of Christ's unlimited power.

In 2 Corinthians 12:10 (NIV), Paul continues by saying, "That is why, for Christ's sake, I delight in weaknesses, in insults, in hardships, in persecutions, in difficulties. For when I am weak, then I am strong." Paul does not limit the scope of weaknesses. He includes every possible thing we might encounter on a day-to-day basis— insults, hardships, persecutions, difficulties. They do not merely refer to our personal failures or physical weaknesses. They cover anything that wears on our self-esteem and self-worth. They encompass all the thoughts that keep us awake at night, battling the hurt, frustration, and confusion caused by life situations.

We must constantly be aware that *each* of our weaknesses has the potential of becoming one of our strengths. God assured the children of Israel, "I am the Lord your God, who holds your right hand, Who says to you, 'Do not fear, I will help you'" (Isaiah 41:13, NASB). Likewise, He is eager to help His children today, assuring us that we have nothing to fear and reminding us that His strength will help us make it through our weakest moments.

When physical problems cause the darkest hours of night to be unbearable, set every pain and every frightening fear in the Father's hands. When frightening thoughts grip your soul at night, claim God's promise that He *is* right there to hold your hand and to remove every fear and concern. Your weakest, most frightening moments are truly your strongest when you allow God to saturate them with His power, peace, and confidence. Then you can safely rest as Christ's power dissolves every fear and gives ultimate strength to replace your greatest weakness.

Through God we shall do valiantly,
and it is He who will tread down our adversaries.
—Psalm 60:12 (NASB)

All it takes is one failure or presumed failure to cause others to forget the hundreds of good things someone has done. Human eagerness to magnify others' faults to discredit them is certainly not reflective of the heart of our loving God and Savior.

When we are the victim of false attacks, how do we react? We often spend sleepless hours, mentally hashing over the events, using select angry thoughts to fight back as we inwardly demand fair treatment. If the accusations were true, we mentally lash back, insisting and even judging that if the accuser is truly a Christian, he/she would forgive.

What is wrong with these scenarios? First, such reactions are never justified in the life of a believer. Spreading gossip, defaming another's character, refusing to forgive or responding in anger never accomplishes God's purposes. Neither does it allow us to reflect our Father's heart.

A woman recently shared that her husband refused to attend church because of a deep hurt caused by another believer in a position of authority. Her spouse was very adamant about never wanting to be around the one who had caused such pain.

Before we criticize either person, we must ask how often we avoid, shun or ignore someone who has offended us. On the other side, do we go about our church or Christian responsibilities, pretending we have not caused harm when we know we have hurt someone?

I must confess, I am as guilty as the next person when it comes to reacting inappropriately and not consistently showing God's love.

However, I *do not* want to stay that way. I really want a change of heart that reflects my Heavenly Father's heart. How can that happen?

- First, I must take full responsibility for *my* actions and attitudes, asking God's forgiveness (1 John 1:9).
- Next, I must ask God if there is someone to whom I need to go to make things right (Matthew 18). If there is, I must focus on *my* wrongdoing (not theirs) and ask forgiveness. Their acceptance or rejection is not my responsibility. I must go in love, doing what God asks.
- I need to embrace the fact that it is only through God that I can find the boldness and courage to do what is needed (Psalm 60:12).
- If I have been offended, I need to offer forgiveness whether the offender asks for it or not. Again, I am only responsible for myself and the attitudes of *my* heart. God will only forgive me as I forgive others (Matthew 18:21–35).
- I must not revisit the wrong done. God removes our sins as far as the east is from the west (Psalm 103:12). I, too, must do the same for others.
- If someone is "impossible to forgive," I need to ask God to help my unforgiving spirit just as the man asked Jesus to help his unbelief (Mark 9:24).

Through God, we will find boldness and courage to do what is right. Then we can sleep, knowing our failures and those of others are a thing of the past. God will take care of any opposition that remains, allowing us to have His kind of victory.

Who shall separate us from the love of Christ? Shall
tribulation, or distress, or persecution, or famine,
or nakedness, or peril, or sword? ...But in all these
things we overwhelmingly conquer through Him
who loved us. For I am convinced that neither
death, nor life, nor angels, nor principalities, nor
things present, nor things to come, nor powers,
nor height, nor depth, nor any other created
thing, shall be able to separate us from the love
of God, which is in Christ Jesus our Lord.
—Romans 8:31–39 (NASB)

Do you have nights when you finally fall asleep only to find yourself doing battle in your dreams? Perhaps the dangers at war in your mind abruptly awaken you, causing you to experience the reality of the evil powers seeking to disrupt your rest. You pray, claiming Jesus's power and victory over every aspect of your being because you *are* God's child. You immediately pray over your family, your neighbors, your church, your job, your colleagues and all that concerns you.

Despite your efforts, your human nature wonders if you have done enough—if your faith will be enough to overcome the terror Satan wants to instill. You remind yourself that "we are *more* than conquerors *through Him* who loved us" (Romans 8:37). You embrace the fact that you do not have to be afraid because God protects His children and gives strength when one takes refuge in Him (Psalm 46:1–3).

Our minds can recall scripture that addresses our problems, yet we often find ourselves continuing to fight one battle after another: low self-esteem, abusive relationships, health issues, limited finances, spiritual dryness, career frustrations, unexpected retirement, etc. Any of these factors can redefine life's direction and purpose, multiplying anxieties that bring sleepless nights. Regardless of the nature of the battle, we need to develop the discipline evidenced by godly men in scripture—always return to God, having full confidence in His directions. Stand firmly by His promises to claim and His actions to take:

- Remember… God's thoughts toward you are precious and outnumber the sand (Psalm 139:17–18).
- His plans are for your welfare, not calamity (Jeremiah 29:11).
- God will forgive you when you confess all known sin to Him (1 John 1:9).
- God is *not a God of confusion but of peace* (1 Corinthians 14:33).
- Submit to God, resist the devil and he will flee from you (James 4:7).
- Trust God with *all* your heart and don't lean on your own understanding; in *all* your ways acknowledge Him and He will make your paths straight (Proverbs 3:5–6).
- Firmly hold on to the fact that absolutely *nothing* can separate you from God and His love for you (Romans 8:38–39).
- Rest in His promise that *He will teach and instruct you in the way you should go, counseling you with His eye upon you* (Psalm 32:8).
- Steadfastly believe that "*nothing is too difficult for God*" (Jeremiah 32:17).

No one and nothing is more loving or powerful than God. Glue these facts to the depths of your soul. Then find calm refuge in your loving Father who promises to keep you safe (Psalm 4:8).

I sought the Lord, and He answered me;
He delivered me from all my fears.
                                    —Psalm 34:4 (NIV)

Job was a righteous man who chose to follow and obey God. No doubt God's faithful protection helped Job know he could count on God regardless of what happened. When Job began to lose everything, some of his friends said it had to be the consequence of sin. They falsely judged Job for things that never crossed his mind or never happened.

Do you ever find yourself in a similar predicament—being falsely accused of something you never considered or did? Do tragic things happen that cause you to reexamine your soul, seriously questioning *why*? Although it is imperative to take personal responsibility for any wrongdoing, negative events are not always an indicator of personal sin. Many do daily battles with physical and/or emotional issues that haunt the darkest hours of night; yet, close examination reveals no indication of underlying sin.

Jesus Himself points out that God allows the sun to shine on the evil and the good, and it rains on both the unrighteous and the righteous (Matthew 5:45). The Old and New Testaments state that God is not one to show partiality (Deuteronomy 10:17, Acts 10:34); therefore, all can expect to experience both good and bad regardless of the degree of personal faithfulness to God.

While God is faithful to reward those who obey Him, one must also consider that Christ followers are often most effective when they can share lessons learned from firsthand experience. This does not mean one has to be an addict to understand the battle of addiction. However, God sometimes allows the believer to experience equally intense and parallel situations so he/she can learn firsthand how God provides deliverance from extreme bondage.

Although Job was experiencing some of the darkest days of his life, he says in Job 12:22 (NASB): "He reveals the deep things of darkness and brings deep shadows into the light." Job had no explanation for the loss of his children, possessions and health; yet he remained confident that his God would bring it to light. He knew from personal experience that there was no reason to doubt his God.

When Daniel and all the wise men of Babylon were sentenced to die if they did not interpret King Nebuchadnezzar's dreams, Daniel expressed that same confidence, saying, "He reveals deep and hidden things, He knows what lies in darkness, and light dwells with Him" (Daniel 2:22, NASB). Therefore, instead of panicking, Daniel found his friends, and they prayed (Life Application Study Bible 1368). When they prayed, God gave the needed answers to interpret the troubling dreams and spare the men's lives.

Job and Daniel were surrounded by seemingly hopeless situations, but their faith-filled attitudes enabled them to know their God would answer. Likewise, God will do the same for you when you choose to trust Him. When heart-rending events happen, do the following:

- Seek the Lord because He knows what is going on, and He *will* answer (Psalm 34:4).
- Do not panic or give in to despair. Find godly friends and ask them to pray with you.
- Praise God for removing the overpowering darkness, allowing you to find rest.

When you trust God during your darkest moments, He will enable you to sleep soundly. He will also bring healing and restoration to your broken, frightened heart as He sheds light on all that lurks in the darkness, giving new hope for the days ahead.

This is the day the Lord has made; let
us rejoice and be glad in it.
—Psalm 118:24 (HCSB)

Many things are "givens" in life. They are concepts we expect anyone to know and understand without explanation. They are principles so fundamental even a child understands with little or no instruction.

Sometimes God speaks, and we treat His words as if they are "givens," brushing them aside as too basic and elementary. Our hearts become indifferent to their truths because we have heard them so many times.

It is easy to treat Psalm 118:24 with casual acknowledgment as many learn the verse as a child. After hearing it year after year, the words seem to lose meaning, just becoming a set of words we can easily recite. Consequently, we begin to overlook the depth and span of their insight.

Take a moment to consider what the words say. They are so simple yet so profound: "This is the day the Lord has made; let us rejoice and be glad in it" (HCSB).

A day does not merely refer to daylight hours. It is one of those "givens." It is the full twenty-four-hour period governing day *and* night. God desires that we rejoice and be glad in *all* of it—even those worrisome nighttime hours. Why do we find this to be hard?

We forget that we live in a creation under constant satanic attack. Those attacks often leave us with pain, disease, grief, anger, confusion, brokenness and other challenges which try to rob our joy day and night. Although David encountered many of the same challenges, his response was that he would rejoice and be glad in the entire twenty-four hours simply because God made it. We would do well to do the same simply because God has given us one more day of life.

When that "one more day of life" finds us unable to sleep due to concerns that weigh heavily on our hearts, we need to remember Paul's command in Philippians 4: 4, 6 (NIV): "Rejoice in the Lord *always*. I will say it again: Rejoice! Do not be anxious about anything, but in every situation, by prayer and petition, with thanksgiving, present your requests to God."

The most powerful and effective help is ours simply by going to our Heavenly Father. His answer might not be what we expect but notice His promise in Philippians 4:7 (NIV): "And the peace of God, which transcends all understanding, will guard your hearts and your minds in Christ Jesus."

David also assures us that in God's presence is *"fullness* of joy" (Psalm 16:11). In other words, nothing is lacking in the joy God gives when we enter His presence for help. Spending time in His presence enables us to shift our fear-ridden thoughts from defeat and despair to joy and hope.

When life's problems are devastating and hard to handle, we must take our eyes off Satan's attacks, taking refuge in God. In His presence, we will discover the joy needed to equip us for rejoicing and being glad regardless of the trials we encounter. Focus on God's eagerness to help, "casting the whole of your care [all your anxieties, all your worries, all your concerns, once and for all] on Him, for He cares for you affectionately and cares about you watchfully" (1 Peter 5:7, Psalm 55:22, AMPB).

Behold, I am the Lord, the God of all flesh;
is anything too difficult for Me?
—Jeremiah 32:27 (NASB)

We are *so* blessed to have a God for whom nothing is too difficult. When creation experiences extreme drought, He can send rain. When people are hungry, He can send food. When finances are depleted, He can send income. When children are in danger, He can give protection. When jobs "play out," He can provide employment. When health is deteriorating, He can heal. When disaster strikes, He can give hope. When nights seem endless, He can give rest.

Perhaps you are thinking, "Wait just a minute. I have had —— happen, and God certainly didn't intervene!" Yes. Sometimes it seems He turns a deaf ear, but remember God's loving reminder: "For My thoughts are not your thoughts, and your ways are not My ways" (Isaiah 55:8, HCSB). Often we are so focused on what *we* want that we forget God might have a better plan.

When He says "no" or "not yet," that does not mean God has abandoned us. Sometimes He is waiting on the best time for all involved. Other times, He is waiting for things to fall in place so it is obvious *He* is the one intervening.

Some days, answers are delayed because God is waiting on us to have a right heart. Psalm 66:18 (NASB) says, "If I regard wickedness in my heart, the Lord will not hear." However, when we confess and turn away from wrong actions and attitudes, God will forgive and answer (1 John 1:9). This allows the opportunity for all to see His eagerness to forgive, His willingness to help and His power to answer. The answer might not be what we expected, but God always has our best interests at heart.

Four months before our fourth child was due, it became obvious he would not make it full-term. We were on vacation and over four hundred miles from home when I had to be admitted to the hospital. The admitting obstetrician told me I would be there till our son's birth. Meanwhile, they would do everything possible to buy some time as he scarcely weighed a pound.

The medical team prepared me for the worst-case scenario, but daily encouraged me by sharing stories of preemie successes. Family and friends faithfully prayed, and day after day, God did things we never anticipated. Less than six weeks later, they had to deliver our son two and a half months early. After a two-week stay in NICU, we were able to take our four-pound, twelve-ounce baby home. Today, he is a healthy young man who recently finished his bachelor's degree.

Many stories could be told of things God did during those five and a half weeks. Of greatest importance is the fact that despite the seemingly impossible situation, God proved *nothing* is too difficult for Him. He not only provided help for my husband and our three young children, but He also restored order when things seemed out of control. When the enormous hospital bills began to arrive, God provided the means to pay them. During the darkest nights, He brought peace and rest. Through the most difficult days, God insured our son's health and well-being.

What is your impossible situation? What seems beyond anyone's ability to help? Are your nighttime hours bombarded with anxieties that seem to have no solution? Does reality indicate you will soon see your heavenly home? Trust God regardless of the outcome. He will hold you securely and will take care of your precious family and friends. He truly is the Lord, the God of all flesh, and *nothing* is too difficult for Him.

The Lord will accomplish what concerns me.
—Psalm 138:8 (NASB)

Unclear purpose, dead-end jobs, difficult relationships, forced retirement, declining health, financial debt—the list seems endless and often repetitive. Regardless of our efforts, something always seems to disrupt the direction we thought we were to take. Intense frustration and restless nights result, leaving a multitude of unanswered questions about the future.

We often overlook one of the most reassuring promises from God Himself: He promises *He* will accomplish what concerns each of us individually. He did not throw us into the complexities of life and expect us to make it on our own. Instead, He gives promise after promise of things *He* is going to do for us individually if we will simply obey and trust Him.

No doubt, God has used different scriptures from time to time to give you reassurance and instruction. If you have not already done so, look them up and write them down. Keep a running list of the scripture promises God has given *you* over the years. Leave room to add to your list.

Especially note *Who* consistently carries out the promises: "The LORD will accomplish what concerns me." This does not mean we are to sit around and do nothing. Instead, we are to obey God's directives, faithfully doing what He says. He, in turn, will personally take care of fulfilling His promises.

Some of the verses possibly on your list might include:

- *God's* thoughts toward you are precious and outnumber the sand (Psalm 139:17–18).

- *His* plans are for your welfare, not calamity (Jeremiah 29:11).
- *He* will forgive your sin when you confess it (1 John 1:9).
- *God* is not a God of confusion but of peace (1 Corinthians 14:33).
- *God* will cause Satan to flee when you submit to God and resist the devil (James 4:7).
- When you trust God with *all* your heart and do not lean on your own understanding, acknowledging Him in *all* your ways, *He* will make your paths straight (Proverbs 3:5–6).
- *He* promises to teach and instruct you in the way you should go, counseling you with *His* eye upon you (Psalm 32:8).
- *He* can do anything needed because "nothing is too difficult for God" (Jeremiah 32:17).
- *God* alone keeps you safe so you can lie down in peace and sleep (Psalm 4:8).
- "Faithful is He who calls you and *He* also will bring it to pass" (1 Thessalonians 5:24, NASB).

When the direction you need to take is unclear, trust God to direct your steps. He does not play mind games. Neither does He "toy" or play with your life. He *wants* to help you discover and accomplish His purposes for you.

When you lie awake puzzling over what to do, allow God's Word to calm your fears and redirect your steps. Be assured of the fact that God Himself is at work on your behalf. He will skillfully guide you through any detours so they will work for your good. Confidently relax and rest in Him as He restores the calm needed to sleep peacefully while God Himself makes His purposes for your life a clear reality.

While I live will I praise the Lord;
I will sing praises unto my God
while I have any being.
　　　　　　　　　　—Psalm 146:2 (KJV)

Have you reached the last inch of life and feel you have nothing left? Perhaps things have deteriorated physically, emotionally and/or financially to the point there literally seems to be nothing that can be done. As you turn to God, there is not enough energy to even ask for help. Nothing but total depletion is left. Is there anything that can be done, *or* is everything truly finished?

First, realize you are not the first person to reach a point of total despair. According to many different scriptures, David himself frequently felt hopeless and discouraged to the point of feeling as if all he had left was breath itself. People found fault with his leadership, attacking him on every side. Their gossip and accusations multiplied his anxiety as others eagerly believed the lies and misrepresentations. His own son went behind his back to undermine David's authority and to instigate a rebellion to overthrow his father. Despite what was going on and how David felt, his faith in God remained steady.

After acknowledging all that was culminating in his hopeless despair, note the response of David's heart: "While I live will I praise the Lord; I will sing praises unto my God while I have any being." It was as if David were saying, "A lot might be wrong, but as long as I have even a mere breath, I will praise the Lord." What a perfect example of what we can do when we feel we have nothing left: "While I have any being, I will praise the Lord."

Praising the Lord does not require extra skill or abilities. Neither does it necessitate energy or health. All it requires is turning sincere thoughts to our Lord to offer praise and thanks to Him.

Perhaps you are thinking, "It also says David sang praises to God. I cannot carry a tune in a bucket!" While that may be true, you can "sing" with your heart. No melody is expected.

One of our most faithful choir members is an "uncertain singer," but he thoroughly enjoys trying. He also sings from his heart. It is better to have a choir full of eager uncertain singers who sing from their heart than a choir full of professional singers who only know the mechanics, not the message of the song. It is okay if you cannot sing. God is only concerned with your heart.

Again, praising God is simply a matter of choice. You can choose to remain defeated because of extreme misfortune, *or* you can choose to give praise to God despite adverse circumstances. That choice will directly affect the outcome and will affect the influence of your life on others.

When others turn against you, leaving you to hurt and grieve over their actions, turn your heart to praise the One who has the answers you need. If you have failed miserably, take ownership of it and return to praising God. In the darkest hours of night when all you have left is one small breath, use it to praise the Lord, who gave His last breath so you could have eternal life with Him. Regardless of what your human nature desires, allow your spirit to praise the Lord!

Only be strong and very courageous… This book
of the law shall not depart from your mouth,
but you shall meditate on it day and night, so
that you may be careful to do according to all
that is written in it; for then you will make your
way prosperous, and then you will have success.
Have I not commanded you? Be
strong and courageous!
—Joshua 1:7, 8–9 (NASB)

When God chose Joshua to take Moses's place, he was not an experienced, seasoned leader. Neither was Joshua confident he could lead two and a half million people because God told him three different times to "be strong and courageous" (Joshua 1:6–7, 9). God promised to be with him and gave Joshua a formula for success. However, God's first and last directions were to be strong and courageous. Strength and courage were essential to successfully leading God's people. The steps of action were sandwiched between these directives.

Is there a major job or task to which God has called you? Do you feel uncertain or doubtful you can do it? Do you lose sleep worrying over your ability to do the job? God's first advice to Joshua was to be strong and courageous. We too must be strong and courageous when God calls us to a given task. That strength and courage is not due to what *we* can do but rests in the fact that God Himself is with us to help.

After reminding Joshua that a mind-set of strength and courage was essential, God then gave His steps of action that would help Joshua effectively lead the Israelites:

- Never let God's Word depart from your lips.

- Meditate on it day and night.
- Be careful to do all that it says.

If Joshua did each of these things, God promised he would have prosperity and success. However, God reminded Joshua one more time: "Have I not commanded you? Be strong and courageous! Do not tremble or be dismayed, for the Lord your God is with you wherever you go" (Joshua 1:9, NASB).

When God blesses you with the opportunity to do a seemingly impossible task, do what He told Joshua: "Be strong and courageous." Do not focus on all the reasons you are *not* qualified for the job. Instead, be strong and courageous in the fact that God Himself called you. Furthermore, He is going to be with you wherever you go, never leaving or forsaking you.

When anxiety interferes with your chance to rest, intentionally replace your sleepless hours with God's steps of action, meditating on His Word day *and night*. Establish your game plan, keeping your Bible nearby so you have easy access to God's Word in the middle of the night. Meditate on its timeless truths. They will not only soothe your worried soul, but they will also direct your uncertain steps. Be strong and courageous as you move forward.

He who digs a pit will fall into it,
And he who rolls a stone, it will come back on him.
—Proverbs 26:27 (NASB)

Sometimes life rocks along, and things seem to be going well. You finally reach a point of relaxing and enjoying life. Every moment, you are grateful for all God is doing. Then it happens. Someone deliberately "digs a pit" or "rolls a stone" to discredit or hurt you, misrepresenting the intent of your heart. They attack you, finding fault with things that never entered your mind. According to these people, you are not good enough, and you fall short of what they want. If they could get away with removing you from the picture, they would do so and never regret it. Their meanness of spirit seems to want to take you down however possible.

At the same time, they speak smoothly to others, giving a surface appearance that everything is great between you. Day and night, you stress over the evil treatment and its unfairness. What can you do?

First, look at your own heart and let God examine it. Allow Him to do what David asks in Psalm 139:23–24 (NASB)—"Search me, O God, and know my heart, try me and know my anxious thoughts, and see if there be any hurtful way in me, and lead me in the everlasting way." Second, if you discover anything that needs to be addressed in your own actions and attitudes, take care of it, allowing God to show you exactly what to do.

When you find nothing wrong, realize God sometimes allows things to happen to see if our hearts are fully and completely His. God allows certain circumstances to see what our choice will be— God's way or man's way. Other times, He allows problems to prevent our becoming spiritually complacent and comfortable. He knows complacency blinds us to certain sins, causing us to cease "fine tuning" our character, motives, thoughts and actions.

When nighttime thoughts battle frustration over another's actions, remind yourself that Satan is the enemy, not people. He likes nothing better than causing trouble between people (especially Christians) when *he* is really the source of the problem. James 4:7 (KJV) says, "Submit yourselves therefore to God. Resist the devil, and he will flee from you."

Also rest in the fact that "'no weapon that is formed against you shall prosper; and every tongue that accuses you in judgment you will condemn. This is the heritage of the servants of the Lord, and their vindication is from Me,' declares the Lord" (Isaiah 54:17, NASB). You might not see God's vindication, but you can be certain He will take care of the situation.

Finally, always be mindful that you are only responsible for *your* thoughts and behavior. When someone "digs a pit" or "rolls a stone," it is better to check your own heart rather than strike back or seek revenge. If there is to be any wrongdoing, leave it with those digging the pit and rolling the stone. Align your thoughts and actions with those of your Lord who left vengeance in the hands of His Father.

Others may be self-satisfied, thinking they successfully put you in your place; but if your heart is right before God, He will take care of those digging the pits and rolling the stones. Just as the Lord fought for the children of Israel while they kept silent (Exodus 14:14), He will do the same for you when you are obedient to do what He asks. Lie down and sleep, confident in your God, who will deliver you and protect you.

As for you…know the God of your father;
And serve Him with a whole
heart and a willing mind;
For the Lord searches all hearts,
And understands every intent of the thoughts.
If you seek Him, He will let you find Him;
But if you forsake Him, He will reject you forever.
Consider now, for the Lord has chosen you…
Be courageous and act.
—1 Chronicles 28:9–10 (NASB)

David instructed his son, Solomon, to know and serve God with his whole heart. He also reminded Solomon that God searches everyone's heart and understands every intent of one's thoughts. David said if Solomon would seek God, he would find Him, but warned of God's rejection should Solomon choose to forsake God. He then affirmed that God Himself had chosen Solomon to rebuild the temple. Since the plan originated with God, it was a task that required action, which would show courage in persevering to its completion.

It is interesting to note that David purposely addresses the fact that God understands "every intent of the thoughts." No doubt David knew from personal experience the intense criticisms and false accusations Solomon would receive as he worked to rebuild the temple. Consequently, David reminded Solomon that God would always know the true intent of his thoughts regardless of the accusations of others. He also reminded Solomon that his course of action had to be one of having courage to act (1 Chronicles 28:10).

The fact of God always knowing the intent of a man's thoughts serves as an encouragement to us today. Any opposition that misrepresents the true intent of *our* thoughts and actions has no power over us. The only thing that matters is pleasing God with the right attitudes of mind and heart, obeying what He says to do.

Do you ever lose sleep over someone who exaggerates or embellishes things you say or do, totally twisting your intent to be something you never considered? Like Solomon, do you face the temptation to let the false accusers distract you from the job at hand?

Encountering such people from time to time is inevitable. However, it is crucial to stay alert to the fact that Satan is merely using them to cause distractions from the greater task to which God has called you. You can focus on their lies, sacrificing hours of physical rest and emotional energy, *or* you can do what David told Solomon: "Be courageous and act."

Like Solomon, there *is* something God has chosen you alone to do. Consequently, beware of getting sidetracked by anyone who tries to dishearten you with their unwarranted criticisms or distortions of truth. Never hesitate to move forward to do the very things God has directed.

Remember, "nothing is impossible with God" (Luke 1:37). That includes silencing your accusers, helping you forgive them *and* helping you succeed at the task to which you were called. Therefore, take courage in your heart and be unwavering in your obedience. When others attack the intent of your heart, do not let worry and stress replace the peace and confidence needed to rest at night. God knows the truth and is ready to help you succeed. That is all that matters.

The Lord will fight for you while you keep silent.
                                    —Exodus 14:14 (NASB)

Are you experiencing a tough dilemma that is blinding you to God's plan for deliverance? Are you battling a challenge for which there seems to be no answer? When Moses led the Israelites out of Egypt, they saw the massive Egyptian army in pursuit. They were terrified, wishing they had never left Egypt. Moses told them to not be afraid, "the Lord will fight for you while you keep silent" (Exodus 14:14, NASB).

Does your situation bear any similarity to that of the Israelites? Have you followed God only to have everything turn to chaos? Are the results of your obedience causing you to doubt your decision?

Over two million Israelites were safely led out of Egypt. Moses told them, "Remember this day...for the Lord brought you out of here by the strength of His hand" (Exodus 14:13, HCSB). Nevertheless, when they saw the Egyptian chariots coming, the Israelites quickly forgot God, allowing fear to take over.

How often do we do the same? God delivers us time after time only to have us "bail out" when we feel trapped and frightened. We quickly overlook the fact of God's powerful deliverances in the past, neglecting to acknowledge His authority over any obstacle. We also fail to see that He can use those very barriers to deliver us if He so chooses.

The Israelites were trapped between the mountains and the Red Sea. Nevertheless, Moses told them, "Don't be afraid. Stand firm and see the Lord's salvation He will provide for you today" (Exodus 14:13, HCSB). God's battle plan was that *He* would fight the Egyptians and would do so that very day while His children *kept silent* (v. 14). There were more than two million Israelites, but God did not need their help. Once again, He wanted them to see the fact that He, alone, could and would protect them from ultimate destruction (Jeremiah 32:27).

Next, God told them to move forward. When they did, God Himself swept the Red Sea back with a strong wind that made a dry path between walls of water on each side (ch. 13, vv. 21–22). Not only did God use the sea itself to make a way out for the Israelites, but He also used it to destroy *all* of Pharaoh's horsemen and army (ch. 14, v. 28).

What does this tell us today?

- When we face frightening situations, we must stand firm, not giving in to fear.
- The barriers we encounter are often the very tools God plans to use to deliver us.
- We must be quiet and still, allowing God to do the fighting (Exodus 14:14). He, alone, has the power and ability to *totally* take care of our problems.
- Regardless of the walls that stand before us, we must confidently move forward when God says to move.

Not only will God provide a way out, but He will also take care of anything attempting to bring harm. He has a sure plan for deliverance and will fight for us while we keep silent. As a result, we can rest at night, free of fear and concern. There will be no need to constantly look over our shoulder, anticipating the approach of our enemies. God will thoroughly take care of them so we can sleep confidently and securely. Allow your loving God to fight for you while you keep silent.

I will instruct you and teach you
in the way which you should go;
I will counsel you with My eye upon you.
　　　　　　　　　　—Psalm 32:8 (NASB)

Despite one's age, there is often confusion about what to do when one moves from one stage of life to the next. It can foster sleepless nights of concern over the uncertainties and decisions that lie ahead. Fortunately, God purposely plans the existence of each person and knows exactly how to help. However, He always allows everyone the choice to accept or reject His counsel and resources. When you choose to follow God, He has encouraging principles and advice to give you hope for today and the days ahead:

- "'For I know the plans that I have for you,' declares the Lord, 'plans for welfare and not for calamity to give you a future and a hope'" (Jeremiah 29:11, NASB).
- "The mind of man plans his way, but the Lord directs His steps" (Proverbs 16:9, NASB).
- "Faithful is He Who calls you, and He also will bring it to pass" (1 Thessalonians 5:24, NASB).
- "The Lord will accomplish what concerns me" (Psalm 138:8, NASB).
- "Delight yourself in the Lord; and He will give you the desires of your heart. Commit your way to the Lord, trust also in Him, and He will do it" (Psalm 37:4–5, NASB).
- "Do not fear, for I am with you; do not anxiously look about you, for I am your God. I will strengthen you, surely I will help you, surely I will uphold you with My righteous right hand" (Isaiah 41:10, NASB).

- "The Lord's loving kindnesses indeed never cease, for His compassions never fail. They are new every morning; great is Thy faithfulness" (Lamentations 3:22–23, NASB).
- "Do not call to mind the former things or ponder things of the past. Behold, I will do something new. Now it will spring forth; will you not be aware of it?" (Isaiah 43:18–19, NASB).
- "Behold, I am the Lord, the God of all flesh; is anything too difficult for Me?" (Jeremiah 32:27, NASB).

God says *He* will accomplish everything that concerns us. That covers any unexpected event or difficulty. However, the choice remains ours to accept or reject His help. Meanwhile, God is available to act when we are ready, giving us strength to endure life's challenges and deliverance to reach our next destination.

When sleepless nights remind you of all that is uncertain or wrong, turn your focus back to God. Tell Him all that is on your heart, trusting Him to restore rest to your sleepless nights. Above all, never hesitate to let His Word give you comfort and guidance.

Remember, God Himself promises to instruct and teach you in the way you need to go. He, also, promises to counsel you as He watches over you. You are of eternal value to Him. That is why Dad could confidently say, "God has never failed anyone, and He is certainly not going to start with you."

Works Cited

Batterson, Mark. 2010. *Primal: A quest for the lost soul of Christianity.* Multnomah.

Cahn, Jonathan. 2011. *The Harbinger.* Lake Mary, Florida: FrontLine.

Chong, Yinong. 2013. "CDC: Nearly 9 millon Americans use prescription sleep aids." CBS News, August 29, 2013. Accessed February 13, 2013. https://www.cbsnews.com/news/cdc-nearly-9-millon-americans-use-prescription-sleep-aids/.

Consumer Reports. 2016. "Why Americans Can't Sleep," January 14.

Gaultiere, Bill. 2019. "Fear-not-365-days-a-year." Retrieved February 7, 2019. www.soulshepherding.org/fear-not-365-days-a-year.

Illustration: Scripture, Illumination. 2012. Retrieved June 19, 2012. www.preaching.com.

Life Application Study Bible: New International Version. 1991. Carol Stream, Ill.: Tyndale House and Grand Rapids, Mich.: Zondervan.

Maraboli, Steve. 2013. *Unapologetically You: Reflections on Life & The Human Experience.* Port Washington, NY: A Better Today Publishing.

Bible Translations Used

Amplified Bible (AMB)

Holman Christian Standard Bible (HCSB)

King James Version (KJV)

New American Standard Bible (NASB)

New International Version (NIV)

About the Author

Pam Koerner is a native Texan and church staff wife. She and her husband, Gary, have five children and four grandsons. She has BS, BA and MRE degrees from Texas Woman's University and Southwestern Baptist Theological Seminary. She worked with special needs students for nine years and currently works for First Baptist Church and First United Methodist Church, Shallowater, Texas, as their accompanist. She teaches private piano and is a member of the Singing Women of West Texas. She enjoys freelance writing and is an active member of her church's quilting and crochet ministries.

CPSIA information can be obtained
at www.ICGtesting.com
Printed in the USA
LVHW111240120520
655430LV00007B/450